THANKSGIVING WITH JESUS

A 30-DAY DEVOTIONAL CELEBRATING
GRATITUDE AND THANKFULNESS

HOLIDAY CELEBRATION DEVOTIONALS
BOOK 5

PETER DEHAAN

Thanksgiving with Jesus: A 30-Day Devotional Celebrating Gratitude and Thankfulness

Copyright © 2025 by Peter DeHaan.

Holiday Celebration Devotionals, Book 5

Library of Congress Control Number: 2025913428

Published by Rock Rooster Books, Grand Rapids, Michigan

ISBN:

- 979-8-88809-149-4 (ebook)
- 979-8-88809-150-0 (paperback)
- 979-8-88809-151-7 (hardcover)
- 979-8-88809-152-4 (audiobook)

Credits:

- Developmental editor: Julie Harbison
- Copyeditor: Robyn Mulder
- Cover design: Cassidy Wierks
- Author photo: Chelsie Jensen Photography

To Jerry Barrett

Series by Peter DeHaan

Holiday Celebration Devotionals rejoice in the holidays with Jesus.

40-Day Bible Study Series takes a fresh and practical look into Scripture, book by book.

Bible Character Sketches Series celebrates people in Scripture, from the well-known to the obscure.

Visiting Churches Series takes an in-person look at church practices and traditions to inform and inspire today's followers of Jesus.

Be the first to hear about Peter's new books and receive updates at PeterDeHaan.com/updates.

CONTENTS

THANKSGIVING

Several countries around the world have an official Thanksgiving holiday, but not all do. Thanksgiving usually occurs in the fall. For example, the United States celebrates Thanksgiving toward the end of November, and Canada celebrates Thanksgiving in October. The origins of Thanksgiving reflect a gratitude for the fall harvest. A few countries celebrate Thanksgiving earlier in the year, aligned with their first harvest or to embrace spring.

Yet even in countries that don't have a recognized Thanksgiving holiday, many people celebrate it anyway. This may reflect personal gratitude or embrace the traditions of those who do.

The purpose of Thanksgiving varies from a

spiritual time of thanking God for his provisions to a personal time to celebrate with family. Yet whether we thank God for his bounty, are grateful for our family, or both, the notion behind the Thanksgiving observance is heartfelt gratitude.

In this 30-day devotional we'll look at what the Bible reveals about thankfulness and gratitude, directing our appreciation to our Creator and Savior. In doing so, may we praise our Lord for the many blessings he gives us throughout the year. May we thank him for loving us and caring for us. May we approach him with grateful hearts.

Use these reflections in whatever way works best for you. One idea is to read it as a month-long devotional during the month of your Thanksgiving holiday. Another option is to begin it thirty days before your celebration to sharpen your focus and heighten your expectation for what is to come. Alternately, you can start reading on Thanksgiving Day and use it to foster a mindset of gratitude for the next thirty days.

Regardless of how we use this month-long collection of daily meditations, may we embrace God for providing for us, loving us, and caring for us.

Let the celebration of Thanksgiving begin.

DAY 1: FIRSTFRUITS OF THE HARVEST
TODAY'S PASSAGE: EXODUS 23:14–19

Focus verse: "Celebrate the Festival of Harvest with the firstfruits of the crops you sow in your field." (Exodus 23:16)

We see the concept of Thanksgiving in the Old Testament, starting with the book of Exodus. It celebrates the harvest, acknowledging the firstfruits, that is, the initial gathering of the crop.

This occurs in the middle of three celebrations. The first is the Festival of Unleavened Bread (Passover). The last is the Festival of Ingathering, which occurs at the end of the harvest.

Between these two is the Festival of Harvest,

which celebrates the firstfruits of the crop. It's the first time in the year that honors God for the bounty of the land.

In his parable of the growing seed, Jesus explains what happens. A man plants his seed. Then he waits. Night and day, whether he's sleeping or working, the seed sprouts, grows, and produces a crop. It seemingly does this on its own. When it's ripe, the man harvests the field (Mark 4:26–29).

The farmer's job is to plant and harvest. He trusts God for what happens in between. God makes it grow. In acknowledging the firstfruits of the harvest, we thank God for his provisions.

Farmers and homesteaders readily understand this. But many people today are removed from the planting and harvesting of crops.

In this way, praising God for the firstfruits seems distant. If this applies to us, the harvest celebration becomes more of a representation of how God has blessed us. Though we may not plant, we do work in other areas. In most cases, our labor results in a paycheck. We use the money we earn through our work to buy our food from those who grow it. Our work also provides a place for us to live and clothes to wear.

Whether we farm the land or work apart from

it, our labor is a gift from God. Our harvest may be a crop, or it may be a paycheck. Both come from our Lord. We should thank the Almighty for our paycheck, just as farmers thank the Creator for their crop.

In both cases, we should appreciate what we have and be thankful for it. It's disrespectful to God to complain that our harvest isn't greater or our paycheck isn't more.

Solomon writes that whoever loves money never has enough (Ecclesiastes 5:10).

Instead, may we love God and esteem him as providing more than enough for us.

Questions: *How can we better thank God for his provisions in our life? Do we appreciate what we have or complain that we don't have more?*

Prayer: Father God, may we thank you for the material blessings you give us. May we offer them to you as the firstfruits of your provisions. Thank you for loving us and taking care of us.

DAY 2: FIRSTFRUITS FULFILLED
TODAY'S PASSAGE: 1 CORINTHIANS 15:20–28

Focus verse: God chose you as firstfruits to be saved through the sanctifying work of the Spirit and through belief in the truth. (2 Thessalonians 2:13)

Starting with Moses, the celebration of firstfruits endures throughout the Old Testament and continues into the New. Yet a secondary meaning of firstfruits emerges through Jesus.

In this way, firstfruits disconnect from the harvest of crops and instead acknowledge the salvation of souls. What started as a celebration of God's physical provisions in the Old Testament morphs into a celebration of God's spiritual provisions in the New Testament, through Jesus.

Here's how.

Paul, in his letter to the church in Corinth, identifies the resurrected Jesus as the firstfruits of those who have fallen asleep. Just as death entered our world through Adam and Eve's sin, Jesus made us alive when he overcame sin. In a spiritual sense, Jesus is the firstfruits of the harvest that leads to eternity.

To accomplish this, Jesus came to earth and sacrificed himself as the ultimate payment for all the wrong things we have done—and will do. He died so that we may live forever with him and Papa in heaven—in a new heaven and a new earth that he will usher in (Revelation 21:1–3).

Yet there is more.

Not only is Jesus the firstfruits, so are we. Seriously. All who follow Jesus are God's firstfruits too.

Father God chose us to be firstfruits, saved through Jesus and the sanctifying work of the Holy Spirit to all who believe God's truth. There's a lot of profound ideas packed into this one short verse, yet at its most basic level, when we believe in Jesus, we become firstfruits.

Jesus is the first of the firstfruits. Through him we likewise become firstfruits.

As firstfruits, we are given to God, just like the firstfruits in the Old Testament. Both instances are worthy of celebration: first for God's physical provisions, and even more so for our spiritual eternity through Jesus.

This is what it means to be spiritual firstfruits.

Questions: *What does it mean to us to be chosen by God as firstfruits? What should our response be to his selection?*

Prayer: Thank you, Jesus, for dying in our place to restore us into a right and full relationship with the Father. May all we do and say serve as our way of thanking you.

DAY 3: GENEROSITY
TODAY'S PASSAGE: 2 CORINTHIANS 9:6–15

Focus verse: You will be enriched in every way so that you can be generous on every occasion, and through us your generosity will result in thanksgiving to God. (2 Corinthians 9:11)

The context of today's passage is the church in Corinth taking an offering to give to other Jesus followers in need, implicitly the believers in the Jerusalem church, which is undergoing religious persecution and enduring physical hardship. Yet we can also receive Paul's teaching as a general encouragement to us today.

Though Paul is not commanding generosity and

sharing with other Christians, he highly commends it. He promises his audience that God will enrich them so they can be generous in every way. We can likewise receive this promise today.

This concept of generosity harkens back to the Old Testament. God blessed Abraham so that he could bless others (Genesis 12:2–3). Likewise, our heavenly Father blesses us so we can bless others. Given how much he loves us, we should expect nothing less.

Our Lord's blessings on us are not so that we can live a life of ease or amass wealth. His provisions are so that we can share with others. As we do, we honor God, point people to him, and grow his kingdom.

Our generosity also results in our thanksgiving to God. He provides blessings for us to share. He enables us to do so without obligation and under no compulsion. Our gifts to others should flow from a compassionate heart, recalling that Jesus gave us the greatest gift of all. With this in mind, we should want to give to others.

The call is to sow generously. Paul repeats this concept in his letter to the Galatians. Succinctly stated, we reap what we sow (Galatians 6:7).

Though the focus of these passages is on money,

we can also be generous with our time. In a world of lonely people, giving them our attention may mean more than giving them our money.

May God give us eyes to see those in need. May he open our hearts to share generously.

The greatest gift we can share is telling them the good news of Jesus's gift of salvation. In this way, our generosity extends into eternity. This will truly result in thanksgiving to God—for both them and us.

Questions: *Do we sow sparingly or generously? Do we praise God for the blessings he gives us so that we can give to others?*

Prayer: Lord, may we overflow with thanksgiving to you as we are generous to others. Please fill our hearts with a sincere desire to give to those in need.

DAY 4: WORDS OF THANKSGIVING
TODAY'S PASSAGE: EPHESIANS 5:1–4

Focus verse: Nor should there be obscenity, foolish talk or coarse joking, which are out of place, but rather thanksgiving. (Ephesians 5:4)

I n Paul's letter to the church in Ephesus, he tells them to follow Father God's example as his dearly loved children. Furthermore, they are to walk in love the same way that Jesus loved us when he sacrificed himself as an offering to God on our behalf.

Building on this, Paul lists six things we should avoid as God's children who love others as Jesus loves us.

Paul says there shouldn't be even a hint of sexual immorality, any kind of impurity, or greed. These do not align with—and are inappropriate for —the holy people of God.

There should be no obscenity, foolish talk, or coarse joking. These are all out of place as the Father's children and followers of Jesus.

As we consider this list of six things to avoid, it's easy to scan it and pick out the ones that aren't an issue for us. This allows us to conclude we're in good shape. In doing so, however, we can easily overlook the remaining items we may struggle with.

Yet this list isn't to condemn us for our wrong behaviors. Instead, it's encouraging us in what is right. What is this proper action?

It's thanksgiving.

That's it. Paul contrasts thanksgiving against sexual immorality, impurity, greed, obscenity, foolish talk, and coarse joking.

Is Paul suggesting that thanksgiving counters these six negative traits? It seems like a simple prescription, but it might have merit.

If we focus on what we shouldn't do, we merely call attention to wrong behavior. It's like thinking of the foods we shouldn't eat when we're on a diet. That seldom works.

Instead, to counter these six sinful tendencies, we distract ourselves by focusing on thanksgiving. When we do so, the pull to do what is wrong lessens.

What are we to thank God for? Here are some ideas to get us started:

Foremost is our right standing with Papa through our salvation that Jesus provides.

Next consider spiritual blessings, such as a community of like-minded friends who follow Jesus. Another thought is how the Holy Spirit sanctifies us and teaches us.

We should also include physical provisions, such as a job that provides for us financially, a place to live, and the basic needs of life. Everything else is a bonus, which is also worthy of thanking God for.

As we offer our thanksgiving to God, our focus shifts away from what we shouldn't do and toward the blessings from our Lord and Savior.

Questions: *What do we think about offering God our thanksgiving as a way to avoid temptation? How can we better integrate a thankful heart into our everyday lives?*

Prayer: Lord, we confess we don't thank you as much as we should. May we turn our hearts to you in gratitude for who you are and all you've done.

DAY 5: HIS LOVE ENDURES FOREVER
TODAY'S PASSAGE: PSALM 136

Focus verse: Give thanks to the LORD, for he is good; his love endures forever. (Psalm 118:29)

As we covered in yesterday's reading, we should offer God our thanksgiving for our salvation, spiritual blessings, and physical provisions. Not only that, but we can also praise him for who he is. His character, after all, is the source that everything flows from.

Today's focus verse tells us to give our thanks to God. One reason is because he is good. He loves us with a love that never ends. It will last through eternity. His love endures forever.

This idea of God's enduring love repeats

throughout Psalm 136. It opens and closes with commands to give thanks to God. Each of its twenty-six verses reminds us of the promise that his love endures forever.

We are to give thanks to him for he is good, the God of gods, and the Lord of lords. His love endures forever (Psalm 136:1–3).

Our God does great wonders, made the heavens, and created our world. He placed lights in the sky: the sun to give us day and the moon to guide our night. His love endures forever (Psalm 136:4–9).

In days of old, God freed his people from their captors in Egypt. He struck down the firstborn of their enemy and brought his children out with mighty power. His love endures forever (Psalm 136:10–12).

The Almighty divided the Red Sea and gave his people a path through it. He then used it to sweep away the enemy army. His love endures forever (Psalm 136:13–15).

For forty years, he led his people in the wilderness. His love endures forever (Psalm 136:16).

After that, the Lord helped his people conquer the promised land. The Almighty struck down great kings and killed mighty rulers. God overcame the king of the Amorites and the king of Bashan. He gave his people these nations' land as an inheritance. His love endures forever (Psalm 136:17–22).

God's provisions continue to this day. The Lord remembers us when we are down. He frees us from our enemies, and he provides food for his creation. His love endures forever (Psalm 136:23–25).

Because of all these reasons—and many, many more—we give thanks to our Father in heaven, for his love endures forever (Psalm 136:26).

May we give him our thanksgiving and our praise.

Questions: *How can we better give thanks to God for who he is? How should the knowledge that his love endures forever influence how we go about our life?*

Prayer: Father God, thank you for who you are and all that you've done for us. You are truly amazing and worthy of our awe. You are all mighty, all present, and all aware. May we never forget these truths.

DAY 6: IN ALL CIRCUMSTANCES
TODAY'S PASSAGE: 1 THESSALONIANS 5:12–28

Focus verse: Give thanks in all circumstances.
(1 Thessalonians 5:18)

As Paul wraps up his letter to the Thessalonian church, he concludes with a list of final instructions. He gives them over a dozen things to do. With so many to consider, it's hard to know what to focus on. The lengthy list may overwhelm us and paralyze us with indecision. The result could be inaction.

Yet three instructions in the middle of the list stand out. After giving them, Paul writes that doing these things is God's will.

Don't we all want to know God's will? Our only

challenge is to determine if this is God's will for the Thessalonian church or God's will for everyone. Given that these appear as general commands, we'll do well to follow them.

What are these three items? They're short and succinct. We do them because it's God's will.

Rejoice Always: To rejoice means to be joyful and delighted. We must do this in all circumstances. Yet this doesn't mean we must always be happy. Some things make us sad, and it's okay to acknowledge that. Yet even among difficult times, Paul wants us to rejoice. We can do this because we know who we serve, and we know what the outcome will be: eternity in heaven with Father God and Jesus.

Pray Continually: We often restrict prayer to a structured time of presenting our requests to God. We close our eyes and bow our heads. We may even fold our hands. Yet we don't need to adapt a prayer posture to talk with God. As we go about our day, we can keep him in the forefront of it. We can praise him and thank him for all that we encounter. We can breathe a silent request for wisdom whenever we seek clarity. In this way, we can pray continuously.

Give Thanks in All Circumstances: We

should adopt an attitude of thanksgiving in all things. This means *everything*. Whatever befalls us, whether good or bad, we should thank God for it.

It's easy to be thankful during happy times, to see God's hand in our blessings.

Amid difficulty, it's harder to be thankful, but we should try. It is, after all, God's will that we thank him. Remember that regardless of what happens, it could always be worse. That's something to be thankful for—in all circumstances.

More importantly, God is always with us and will never leave us—regardless of our situation. That's another thing to be thankful for.

And when we die, we'll spend eternity with him. Thank you, Jesus!

Questions: *How well do we do at giving thanks in all circumstances? Do we go through life with optimism or pessimism? Which one more honors God?*

Prayer: Holy Spirit, show us how to be thankful in all circumstances. Remove negativity and a critical spirit from us. When things don't go our way, may we rejoice, pray, and give thanks.

DAY 7: SING TO THE LORD
TODAY'S PASSAGE: EZRA 3:7–11

Focus verse: With praise and thanksgiving they sang to the LORD: "He is good; his love toward Israel endures forever." (Ezra 3:11)

The book of Ezra, likely written by the priest and scribe Ezra, opens with the story of Zerubbabel and King Cyrus of Persia. Ezra himself doesn't even show up until chapter seven, two-thirds of the way through the book. We'll cover Ezra in our reading for Day 10.

Our story for today starts with King Cyrus stating that God appointed him to rebuild the temple in Jerusalem (Ezra 1:2). Cyrus issues a decree to that effect. The king permits anyone who wants to return to Jerusalem to go. He also gives them all the temple accessories King Nebuchadnezzar had taken from the temple before he razed it, some seventy years earlier.

Once the people arrive and settle in their towns, their next task is rebuilding the altar so they can resume offering sacrifices. Zerubbabel, one of the many who return, becomes a leader who oversees the process.

A year later, when they turn their attention to rebuilding the temple, Zerubbabel leads this effort. With the foundation of the temple laid—though their work has barely begun—they celebrate their accomplishment. Though we might think it wiser to mark the successful completion of a project, they acclaim a successful start.

Interestingly, this may have been a spontaneous reaction and not a planned celebration. Regardless, God is honored. That's what matters.

Accompanied with praise and thanksgiving, they sing to the Lord: "God is good; his love endures forever."

They give a great shout of jubilation for what has begun and for the outcome they expect. Some people overflow with tears and others overflow with joy. The tumult builds and is so great that others hear it from far away.

Their worship of God is through song. It centers on praise and thanksgiving. They praise the Lord for who he is, a good God who loves them without limit. They give thanks for what they accomplished through him.

In their example, we see we need not wait for the completion of a project to celebrate God. We can also sing our adoration to him at the commencement of a grand undertaking, such as a groundbreaking ceremony.

We can give him our praise and thanksgiving for what he has done. We can likewise give him our praise and thanksgiving for what he has begun. And we can give him our praise and thanksgiving for what he is doing.

May we take every opportunity to do all three. God deserves no less.

Questions: *How prone are we to offer God our praise and thanksgiving? What are some areas where we can do this better?*

Prayer: Father God, open our eyes to see opportunities for us to offer you the praise and thanksgiving you deserve. We ask you, Holy Spirit, to reveal these occasions and guide our worship. We ask this in Jesus's name. Amen.

DAY 8: ALWAYS THANK GOD
TODAY'S PASSAGE: EPHESIANS 1:15–21

Focus verse: I have not stopped giving thanks for you, remembering you in my prayers. (Ephesians 1:16)

A recurring sentiment at the beginning of many of Paul's letters is his declaration that he gives thanks to God for the people he's writing to. How this must encourage his recipients, knowing that their lives and conduct are worthy of the apostle's offering of thanksgiving to their Lord.

Besides Ephesians, we read similar declarations in Paul's letters to the Romans (Romans 1:8), Philippians (Philippians 1:3), Colossians (Colossians

1:3), and twice to the Thessalonians (1 Thessalonians 1:2 and 2 Thessalonians 1:3). Even the church in Corinth, with their many struggles and need for correction, receives this encouraging affirmation (1 Corinthians 1:4).

Not only do these five churches receive this reassuring message, but so do two individuals: Timothy (2 Timothy 1:3) and Philemon (Philemon 1:4).

Paul's thanksgiving of praise commends these churches and individuals for their faith in God and the actions it produces. Yet implicitly, Paul's thanksgiving more so acknowledges God for his grace and mercy given to these people.

We can learn three lessons from Paul's example of giving thanks.

First, we see this as a common expression in his prayer life. He gives thanks to God for those churches and people who are part of his ministry. Though it would be easy to complain to God about their shortcomings, Paul instead thanks God for the results of his work in their lives and the outcomes they produce.

Given Paul's example, who should we thank God for? Consider thanking God for our family and friends. We can thank God for our church and faith community. We can also thank God for other people, both those who mentor us and those we mentor.

But we shouldn't do this once and forget it. It should be an ongoing part of our worship and our prayers. We should never stop thanking God for these people.

Second, as we consider Paul's personal letters to Timothy and Philemon, we can look internally into the conduct of our faith journey. Is our faith—and the outcomes of our faith in action—worthy of other people thanking God for it? We consider this, however, not to evoke a false sense of pride or to produce guilt-paralyzing shame. Instead, the question becomes, do other people see God in our lives? Is what he's doing enough to prompt others to thank him?

Third, we consider Paul's letters to the churches in Rome, Philippi, Colossae, Thessalonica, and Corinth. If Paul heard about the church we attend, would he thank God for it? We ask this question not to commend or condemn our church, but to ensure we're giving God the opportunity to work through us and produce praiseworthy outcomes.

Questions: *Who should we thank God for? Based on Philippians 2:12–13, do we live our lives and work out our salvation in a way that prompts others to thank God for his work in our lives?*

Prayer: Jesus, we thank you for saving us and for your work in our lives to make us more like you. May everything we say and do represent you positively to the world that watches us.

DAY 9: DON'T BE ANXIOUS
TODAY'S PASSAGE: PHILIPPIANS 4:4–9

Focus verse: Do not be anxious about anything, but in every situation, by prayer and petition, with thanksgiving, present your requests to God.
(Philippians 4:6)

We live in anxious times. We have much we can worry about. Yet we shouldn't. Paul writes to the church in Philippi that they should not be anxious about anything. We will do well to embrace this command to counter any worry or anxiety that may have a grip on us.

In view of this, Paul gives a trio of prescriptions

PETER DEHAAN

to deal with the malady of anxiety. They are prayer, petition, and thanksgiving.

By mentioning prayer and petition separately, Paul implies a difference between the two, even though we might at first consider them synonyms.

Prayer is communication with God. It includes praise, confession, and supplication, along with petition and thanksgiving. Ideally, prayer should flow naturally from us as we go about our day. Though we aren't wrong to have prescribed moments of prayer at specific times—such as when we rise, eat, and go to bed—this should not limit when we talk to God.

Petition is a specific subset of prayer. It's interceding on behalf of others. It's not self-focused, which is supplication. Instead, petition looks at the needs of others. When we make requests to God for other people, we remove the attention from ourselves to address what others lack.

The third element of Paul's trio of instructions is thanksgiving, which is another subset of prayer. The opposite of thankfulness is ingratitude. Are we known for being grateful to God for what we have or complaining about our perceived shortfall?

So there is no doubt, the God-honoring reaction

is thanksgiving. We are to have thankful hearts in both our interaction with God and with others.

When we embrace God in prayer, intercede for others, and offer thanksgiving, we remove the focus from ourselves and redirect it to our Lord and to others. Then we are ready to present our requests to God.

This is when we can cast all our anxiety on him, mindful that he cares for us (1 Peter 5:7). He will sustain us and not let us be shaken (Psalm 55:22).

Knowing that the Almighty cares for us, will sustain us, and will not let anything shake us are three more reasons to offer the Lord our thanksgiving.

Questions: *How do we react when anxiety attacks us and attempts to steal our joy? Do we find it more difficult to be thankful to God or thankful to others?*

Prayer: Heavenly Father, when anxiety threatens us, may we respond with prayer, petition, and thanksgiving before we present our requests to you. Turn our attention from ourselves to you and to others. As we do this, cast our anxiety far away.

DAY 10: SONGS OF THANKSGIVING
TODAY'S PASSAGE: NEHEMIAH 12:22–47

Focus verse: Mattaniah, who, together with his associates, was in charge of the songs of thanksgiving. (Nehemiah 12:8)

The Bible tells us about the exiles who return to Jerusalem. The wall around the city is in shambles. They need to rebuild it. The man who leads the rebuilding project is Nehemiah.

In rebuilding the wall, Nehemiah encounters opposition and confronts forces who want to keep him from completing his mission. Yet he persists, and God provides. Though the wall had been in a broken-down state for decades, under Nehemiah's leadership—and with God's provision—the people rebuild the wall in only fifty-two days. It's a remarkable feat, with the credit rightly going to God for his protection and blessings.

Once completed, they have a dedication ceremony to celebrate the accomplishment. As part of their festival, they sing songs of thanksgiving. This isn't a singular song of praise, but there is more than one song, likely many. These songs of thanksgiving are a central part of their dedication ceremony.

Though the Bible doesn't tell us the words to any of these songs of thanksgiving, we can imagine them as overflowing with worship of God and praise for his provisions.

From a physical standpoint, the wall represents safety from their enemies. It stands as a barrier to keep out any who would want to attack them and cause harm. From a psychological viewpoint, the wall shows the restoration of Jerusalem as a city— and symbolically the nation that once was. From a spiritual perspective, the restoration of the wall symbolizes God's re-acknowledgment of them as his people.

Physical safety, psychological encouragement,

and spiritual restoration are all worthy reasons to offer songs of thanksgiving to God.

These songs occur in a planned dedication ceremony. But we need not have a formal structure to sing songs of thanksgiving to our Lord. Our songs can be informal, and they can be spontaneous. The main thing is that they come from our heart.

Our songs of thanksgiving can emerge because of a major accomplishment or acknowledge a smaller event—even a seemingly trivial one.

We can sing our songs of thanksgiving as part of a group effort or on our own as a private concert to an audience of one: Our Lord.

He is worthy of our praises and our songs of thanksgiving.

Questions: *What songs of thanksgiving should we sing to God today? Does God want us to sing to him if we don't have a nice voice or can't carry a tune?*

Prayer: Lord, may we be ever mindful to sing songs of thanksgiving to you as we go about our day. Whether impressive or pitiful, may you receive our singing as a sincere offering of gratitude for who you are and what you've done.

DAY 11: THANKSGIVING MADE FOR ALL

TODAY'S PASSAGE: 1 TIMOTHY 2:1–4

Focus verse: I urge, then, first of all, that petitions, prayers, intercession and thanksgiving be made for all people. (1 Timothy 2:1)

I n writing to his protégé Timothy, Paul urges us to make petitions, prayers, intercession, and thanksgiving for all people. Though we could dismiss this as a personal instruction that applies only to Timothy, we're wise to embrace it as applying to us too.

Paul urges four activities: petitions, prayers, intercession, and thanksgiving. We may think of prayers, petitions, and intercession as synonyms. If we do, may the threefold repetition emphasize the importance of prayer.

Yet we can also look at each word for its subtle difference. In general, prayer is talking with God. We should talk with God about all people. Next, when we petition God on behalf of them, we seek his grace and his mercy in response to their shortcomings. Third is intercession. It's more intense. We plead on behalf of all people. This is what Abraham did for the citizens of Sodom (Genesis 18:22–33).

The fourth element of Paul's urging is thanksgiving. At first, thanksgiving seems out of place with the trio that precedes it. But Paul is intentional about including thanksgiving. Just as we should pray, petition, and intercede for everyone, we should likewise give thanks for all people.

It's not challenging to be thankful for people we love, respect, or admire. But we push back at giving thanks to God for those we dislike, disregard, or renounce.

Yet Paul includes these individuals in his instruction that we make thanksgiving for all people. All means all.

Specifically, we're to pray and give thanks for our government and those in authority over us.

This is easy when we like those in power, but it's much harder when we dislike them or disagree with them—especially when we see them opposing God.

Yet *all people* means all people, every one of them. Jesus does, after all, tell us to love our enemies and pray for those who oppose us (Matthew 5:44). In this regard, Paul merely urges us to do what Jesus has already commanded.

It may help to realize that no person is completely righteous, nor is anyone completely evil. Though the proportions differ, everyone has strengths and weaknesses. We should give thanks for whatever good we see in each person.

In response to Jesus's work in our lives, may we say prayers of thanksgiving for all people.

Questions: *Who do we struggle to pray and thank God for? What must we do to correct our shortcomings?*

Prayer: Jesus, may we love everyone just as you love us. When offering prayers of thanksgiving for those we don't like, please show us your perspective. Then give us the strength and willingness to thank you for them—every one of them.

DAY 12: REGARDLESS OF THE SITUATION

TODAY'S PASSAGE: ROMANS 14:1–10

Focus verse: Whoever eats meat does so to the Lord, for they give thanks to God; and whoever abstains does so to the Lord and gives thanks to God. (Romans 14:6)

We may think today's focus verse addresses being a vegetarian. It does not, at least not directly. The context is about eating meat offered to idols.

Idol worship was a huge issue during the time of the early church. Though we still may worship idols today, they are not physical idols we bow before and sacrifice animals to. Today's idols are figurative. We worship them with our time and attention, giving them priority in our lives, which pulls us away from God and dishonors him.

Some followers of Jesus felt it was wrong to eat meat sacrificed to idols. In their mind, this aligned them with the pagan practice and gave these false gods credibility. Therefore, as a matter of conscience, they declined to eat the meat of animals sacrificed to these inert statues. They gave thanks to God for the food they ate, which didn't come from idols.

Conversely, other followers of Jesus had no qualms about where their meat came from. They were not offering animal sacrifices to idols. They were not taking part in the ceremony. By eating the meat afterward, they did not see themselves as endorsing the idol it came from. They gave thanks to God for their meat and savored it.

The result—which is too often the case when people disagree about spiritual practices—was to judge the other group. Each side looked down on the people whose practice didn't align with theirs. They treated them with contempt.

With pride, each group held their heads high over their conclusion on how to handle this contentious matter. With smug conviction, they dismissed those who held the opposite view. They judged the other with wrong motivations, dishonoring God in the process.

Today we seldom consider eating meat sacrificed to idols. Yet many other issues have arisen in how we practice our faith and worship our Lord. To all these, we must apply Paul's instructions about eating idol-sacrificed meat to today's issues of faith. We honor God when we do so.

Back to our discussion of vegetarians. If you're a vegetarian, don't criticize those who eat meat. And if you eat meat, don't look down on those who abstain. Instead, everyone should thank God for their food and withhold their judgment of others.

This applies to meat and to every other nonessential area of contention. Simply thank God and don't criticize others.

Questions: *When have we wrongly judged someone whose actions didn't align with ours? When have we looked down on another follower of Jesus who held a doctrine different from our own?*

Prayer: Jesus, give us eyes to see others as you see them. Show us how to withhold judgment. Instead, may we give you thanks for your provisions and your blessings.

DAY 13: EVERYTHING GOD CREATED IS GOOD

TODAY'S PASSAGE: 1 TIMOTHY 4:1–5

Focus verse: For everything God created is good, and nothing is to be rejected if it is received with thanksgiving. (1 Timothy 4:4)

In his first letter to Timothy, Paul warns his apprentice about false teaching. Paul foresees a time when people will abandon their faith to follow misguided ideas. Paul uses intense language to describe these misguided teachers. He calls them deceiving spirits who teach the demonic. They are hypocritical liars, with seared consciences. That's strong language.

Paul shares two examples of what they will

teach. One is that they will forbid marriage. The other is that they will order people to not eat certain foods.

God instituted the union of a man and a woman from the very beginning, when he created Adam and Eve. He told them to be fruitful and multiply. God repeated the instruction to Noah after the flood.

Marriage is wonderful. Sex is wonderful. And children are wonderful. God created us to experience all three. He commanded it from the beginning.

To not get married is to miss out on one of God's intended purposes for his children. Though we may choose to follow Paul's example of celibacy, this is the exception and not the expectation. For most of us, we can best honor God by getting married and having children. Yet if we're single with no prospects of marriage, we can likewise choose to honor God through it (1 Corinthians 7:1–11).

Even more so, we should not command people to not marry. God created us to procreate. This should occur within the sacredness of marriage.

The other example of false teaching Paul gives

is telling people to abstain from eating certain foods. Though the Old Testament had strict dietary expectations of what to eat and what not to eat, these no longer apply. Now that Jesus has showed us a better way to approach God in faith, we no longer need to earn our salvation through our actions.

When we believe in Jesus and know the truth, we can receive and eat all foods with thanksgiving. We will, however, do well to focus on consuming what is healthy and minimizing our intake of what is not. Yet through moderation, we can even enjoy our desserts—provided we do so with thanksgiving.

Everything that God created is good. This includes both procreation and food. There's no need to reject either, as long as we receive them with thanksgiving.

Questions: *What is a God-honoring perspective to hold about marriage, sex, and having children? How can we balance eating a healthy diet with embracing all foods with thanksgiving?*

Prayer: Heavenly Father, thank you for how you created us to function. Thank you for the food you've given us to eat. May we celebrate everything you created as good. May we receive it with thanksgiving.

DAY 14: GOD IS GOOD
TODAY'S PASSAGE: PSALM 107

Focus verse: Open for me the gates of the righteous; I will enter and give thanks to the LORD.
(Psalm 118:19)

We don't know who wrote Psalms 107 and 118, but the author (or authors) is intent on praising God with thanksgiving. The phrase *give thanks to the LORD* occurs seven times in these two psalms.

In addition, both psalms begin with the same line, which suggests the same author. This opening refrain is "Give thanks to the LORD, for he is good; his love endures forever."

Though we don't need a reason to proclaim our

thanksgiving to God, this passage provides justification. We give thanks to the Lord because he is good. Let's not rush past this.

Though we may think of some people as being good—and may even think of ourselves as being good—this is incorrect. Though some people can be mostly good, no one is completely good. No one, that is, except for God. Jesus says so (Mark 10:18).

God—and only God—is good. We can count on it. Because of his goodness, we praise him. We give thanks to the Lord, because he is good.

Then we add to his goodness the affirmation that his love endures forever. It's not temporary. It's not even conditional—the result of what we might do or not do. Our Lord's love for us is absolute. It lasts forever. It extends into eternity.

Psalm 107 contains four more instructions to give thanks to God. The same phrase repeats each time. "Let them give thanks to the LORD for his unfailing love and his wonderful deeds for mankind." The fourfold repetition emphasizes the statement's truth to make sure we don't miss it.

Though we don't need a second incentive to give thanks to God, this time the reason is his unfailing love. As we already covered, it's a love that never ends. Another reason in these four verses are his wonderful deeds to us. He loves us and watches over us. He gives us what we need and does wonderful things for us. This is another motivation to offer him our thanksgiving.

There's one more verse in these two psalms about giving thanks to God that we haven't covered. It's today's focus verse.

Among victory and discipline, the psalmist asks God to open for him—or her—the gates reserved for those who are righteous. Upon entering the special place where the righteous gather—perhaps an allusion to heaven—they'll offer thanksgiving to the Lord.

He is good, and his love endures forever.

Questions: *What other reasons are there to offer God our thanksgiving? What do we think of God's goodness and everlasting love?*

Prayer: Jesus, we thank you for loving us and sacrificing yourself to remit the penalty for all the wrong things we've done. Through you we are righteous. We look forward to spending eternity with you in heaven.

DAY 15: GRATITUDE

TODAY'S PASSAGE: COLOSSIANS 3:12–17

Focus verse: And be thankful. (Colossians 3:15)

Paul gives the Colossians several inspiring instructions. The list is both challenging and lofty. Just as they put on their clothes each day, the apostle tells them to wear compassion, kindness, humility, gentleness, and patience. In addition, they're to bear with each other and forgive one another, following the example of Jesus who forgave them of everything they've ever done or ever will do.

They're to cover all this with love, which brings about unity.

That's a lot to take in, but there's more. They're

to let Jesus's love rule their hearts as members of one body, called to live in peace.

The last item of Paul's lengthy list is to be thankful.

They—and we along with them—are to be thankful to God, who calls us to do these things and equips us to accomplish them. Though we will struggle with these items on our own, through God, we can move toward them. This is more than enough reason to be thankful.

Next, Paul moves toward gratitude, which is another word for thankfulness.

To get to gratitude, Paul encourages them to let the good news of Jesus permeate their being. They're to instruct and caution one another in all that is true. They're to use psalms, hymns, and Holy Spirit inspiration to sing to God with heartfelt gratitude.

Yes, our songs to God should overflow with a sincere gratitude. Given that he loves us unconditionally and saved us from our sin so that we can live with him forever, the inescapable conclusion is gratitude. We are thankful to him for who he is and what he does.

Yet Paul's message of thankfulness continues. He says that all the words we speak and all the things we do should be in the name of Jesus as we give thanks to Father God, through his Son and our Savior.

Instead of being overwhelmed by all that Paul expects us to do, we should be thankful that our Lord cares enough for us to call us to do these things. Through God we can do just that.

May we thank the Almighty who desires we pursue these ideals, relying on him to bring us closer to reaching these goals each day as we move closer to him.

Questions: *Does Paul's list encourage us to pursue these items with joy or overwhelm us with the difficulty of accomplishing them? How can we rightly balance these instructions with a call to be thankful and offer gratitude?*

Prayer: Jesus, may we honor you as we go forward under the power of the Holy Spirit to move our lives into alignment with you and your church. As we do so, may we be thankful, sing with heartfelt gratitude, and thank Papa for his work in our lives. Amen.

DAY 16: RESTORATION

TODAY'S PASSAGE: JEREMIAH 30:18–21

Focus verse: From them will come songs of thanksgiving and the sound of rejoicing. (Jeremiah 30:19)

At the time of the prophet Jeremiah, Assyria had already conquered the nation of Israel. They are no more. Though the nation of Judah escaped judgment then, they won't avoid their punishment forever. Babylonia oppresses them, and their end as a nation draws near.

Yet Jeremiah prophesies a future restoration. It's a glorious time when God will reestablish them as a people. In this prophecy, Jeremiah quotes the very words of God.

Our Lord says, "I'll restore the fortunes of Jacob," which represents the nation of Judah. "I'll have compassion on their buildings and will rebuild the city. The palace will again stand."

Though this had not yet happened for the people, when it does, it will be a cause for celebration. Jeremiah continues God's promise by proclaiming that when it occurs, the people will sing songs of thanksgiving, and they will rejoice. Their numbers will grow, and God will honor them.

This forward-looking prophecy of thanksgiving reveals much. Not only can we offer our thanks to God for what he has done and what he is doing, we can also thank him for what he will do.

Here we have God's direct promise, as recorded in Scripture, for the basis of thanksgiving. And there are many more forward-looking promises that are likewise worthy of us giving God our praise. For each one of these, we can sing songs of thanksgiving to our Lord. We should keep this in mind as we read through the words of the prophets, looking for prophecies that warrant us thanking him in praise.

Beyond this, we can also offer songs of thanksgiving for our future. We may have prayed for a certain outcome and received it in faith, even though we have not yet seen it. For this, we can offer God our thanksgiving.

Perhaps we live in hopeful expectation of God's future blessings. We can sing songs of thanksgiving to him now and rejoice for what we have not yet realized, but one day will.

May we sing our Lord songs of thanksgiving and rejoice.

Questions: *What are some of God's promises that warrant offering songs of thanksgiving? How well do we do at thanking God for what has not yet occurred, believing in faith that it one day will?*

Prayer: Lord, may we recall your promises in Scripture so we can thank you. Grant us the faith to praise you for your blessings we haven't yet realized and can only see from afar.

DAY 17: APPOINTED TO SING
TODAY'S PASSAGE: 2 CHRONICLES 20:1–29

Focus verse: Jehoshaphat appointed men to sing to the LORD and to praise him for the splendor of his holiness as they went out at the head of the army, saying: "Give thanks to the LORD, for his love endures forever." (2 Chronicles 20:21)

King Jehoshaphat is worried. Three nations march toward Jerusalem to wage war on him and the nation of Judah. The king knows he's outnumbered. From a human perspective, he and his army can't win.

Logically, he has three options. One is to fight, even though he knows he will lose. Another is to flee for their lives. A third idea is to negotiate a peace treaty. Jehoshaphat does none of these. Instead, he seeks God before he acts.

Jehoshaphat praises the Lord Almighty, presents his concerns, and admits he doesn't know what to do. The king looks to God for a solution.

God's Spirit comes upon Jahaziel. He prophesies and encourages the people. His concluding proclamation is to not fear or be discouraged. They are to face their enemy the next day and trust God for the outcome.

Jehoshaphat bows and worships God. Some of the Levites praise the Lord. They do so loudly.

The next day, as they prepare to engage with the enemy, Jehoshaphat appoints men to sing to the Lord and offer praises. They're even to lead the army into battle. Imagine that, a choir on the front line. They'll surely die when they face the enemy.

Yet this is a human perspective. God has a better plan.

As soon as the men sing their praise of thanks to God, the enemy armies turn on each other. They slaughter one another and die. This spares Jehoshaphat, his army, and the nation of Judah. They didn't even need to fight. The Lord fought on their behalf. All they needed to do was sing their thanksgiving to him.

It takes Jehoshaphat's army three days to gather all the plunder from their fallen enemy. On the fourth day, they praise the Lord.

Jehoshaphat leads the people back to Jerusalem, full of joy. They rejoice in the Lord and praise him. The surrounding kingdoms hear what happened and fear God for what he did.

This all occurred because Jehoshaphat made it a priority to sing thanksgiving to God for his enduring love.

Questions: *How can we better sing to God and praise him? How often do we thank him in advance for what we believe he will do?*

Prayer: Lord, when we face an overwhelming situation, may we not panic. Instead, may we turn to you. When you promise to rescue us, may we give thanks to you in faith for what we believe will happen. We ask this in Jesus's name, amen.

DAY 18: CUP OF THANKSGIVING
TODAY'S PASSAGE: 1 CORINTHIANS 10:14–22

Focus verse: Is not the cup of thanksgiving for which we give thanks a participation in the blood of Christ? And is not the bread that we break a participation in the body of Christ? (1 Corinthians 10:16)

If you're not familiar with the phrase *the cup of thanksgiving*, that's understandable. It only appears once in the Bible. Given its singular occurrence, we can't use other verses to help us understand this passage.

But consider the clues around this phrase. It mentions Jesus's blood, the bread, and the body of Christ. This connects *the cup of thanksgiving* with the

Lord's Supper, also called Holy Communion or the Eucharist (1 Corinthians 11:23–26).

Building on the Passover celebration, Jesus instituted the Lord's Supper with his disciples just before he ransomed himself to restore us to Father God. The Lord's Supper is a celebration of Jesus and what he did to save us.

Each time we share this meal, we remember that Jesus sacrificed himself in our place. In doing so, he reconciled all who believe in him with God the Father. This gives us eternal life, a new perspective that starts on earth today and extends forever into eternity after we die.

The cup of thanksgiving represents all this—and more. Jesus loves us, and Jesus died for us. Jesus heals us, and Jesus saves us. Because of who he is— and what he did—we believe in him and trust him with our souls.

We should ponder all these thoughts the next time we celebrate the Lord's Supper. As we partake of the Communion cup, which represents Jesus's blood and symbolizes his death, we should receive it as a cup of thanksgiving. We drink it as a physical display of thankfulness. We need not say a thing— though we can if we want.

As we do this, we aren't wrong to approach the

Lord's Supper table with a solemn reverence to remember Jesus's sacrificial death. Yet his death is not the end or something for us to mourn. It marks the start of something new. Jesus didn't remain in his grave. He rose from the dead. His resurrection is something for us to celebrate. May we remember this every time we drink from the cup of thanksgiving.

Thank you, Jesus, for loving us, dying for us, and saving us. We lift our cup of thanksgiving to you—for who you are and what you did.

Questions: *How can viewing the Lord's Supper as a cup of thanksgiving impact how we take part in this sacrament? How can we better thank Jesus for loving us, dying for us, and saving us?*

Prayer: Jesus, as we remember you in the sacrament of the Lord's Supper, may we also remember to thank you for dying to save us and resurrecting from the dead to give us eternal life. Thank you, Jesus.

DAY 19: GIVE THANKS TO THE LORD
TODAY'S PASSAGE: 1 CHRONICLES 16

Focus verse: "Save us, God our Savior; gather us and deliver us from the nations, that we may give thanks to your holy name, and glory in your praise." (1 Chronicles 16:35)

The nation of Israel takes the ark of God into battle, and the Philistines capture it (1 Samuel 4:1–10). But the Philistines don't keep the ark, for its presence inflicts whatever town holds it. They eventually send it back to Israel on a cart, and it ends up in Kiriath Jearim, where it stays for twenty years (1 Samuel 7:1–2).

Later, King David tries to bring the ark to Jerusalem, but he stops when the trip goes awry

(1 Chronicles 13). When he realizes what went wrong, he tries again. This time he succeeds (1 Chronicles 15).

This is the background for what happens in today's passage. It's a grand celebration of the ark of God being brought back and placed inside the tent reserved for it, for the temple hadn't been built yet.

David appoints a team of Levites to minister there. They are to extol, thank, and praise God. Asaph leads this effort. Their song of praise reads much like a psalm and parallels Psalm 106.

As instructed by David, this song extols the Lord, offering him praise and thanksgiving. It opens and concludes with the instruction to praise God. It also includes instructions to give thanks to God.

The first time it says to thank the Lord, "for his love endures forever." We covered this phrase extensively in the reading for Day 5, as well as in Days 7, 14, and 17. This phrase occurs over forty times in the Old Testament, most of them in the book of Psalms, so we should be familiar with it.

The second time this song talks about thanking God, it's a future-focused reference. In a prophetic nod, it cries out to God to save them, gather them, and deliver them from their enemies. We will eventually see this fulfilled through Jesus when he gathers his people to save them from the enemy of sin.

Because of God's future rescue, they may give thanks to God, to "give thanks to your holy name."

It's one thing to give thanks to God for his character and his blessings, but to give thanks to his name may seem like a stretch.

Yet even his name is holy. His name is also worthy of receiving our praise and thanksgiving.

May we not only view God as holy but also esteem his name as holy. May we give thanks to his holy name.

Questions: *Why might we want to give thanks to God's holy name instead of just thanking him directly? How can our understanding that God's name is holy influence how we refer to him?*

Prayer: Lord God and Savior, you are holy. May we praise your holy name forever. May we thank your holy name and all that it entails.

DAY 20: ANNA GIVES THANKS FOR JESUS

TODAY'S PASSAGE: LUKE 2:36–38

Focus verse: She gave thanks to God and spoke about the child to all who were looking forward to the redemption of Jerusalem. (Luke 2:38)

Even though Anna only appears in one passage in the Bible—and a short one at that—she emerges as a remarkable woman. First, Luke identifies her as a prophet, a prophetess, if you will. Though there aren't many prophetesses in the Bible, there are some, such as Miriam, Deborah, Huldah, and Philip's four daughters.

By identifying Anna as a prophet, Luke

confirms prophetic ministry isn't just for men, but open to all people. Anna exemplifies that.

We also know she is old. Luke writes "very old." Anna had only been married for seven years when she became a widow. She didn't remarry and had been a widow ever since. She's now eighty-four. Some translations of the Bible say that she had been a widow for eighty-four years, which would make her even older—likely over one hundred.

Anna has a deep commitment to God—extremely so. Luke writes she never leaves the temple. She worships day and night, fasting and praying. This characterization is hyperbole to make a point. She'd surely leave the temple to sleep. And she couldn't fast continuously; she'd have to eat at some point. Yet this shouldn't distract from the conclusion that she's dedicated to God and worships him with all her being.

Anna's at the temple—as we'd expect—when Jesus's parents arrive to undergo the purification rights that Moses prescribed (Leviticus 12:1–4). The righteous and devote Simeon approaches them and praises God for Jesus and what he will do (Luke 2:25–35).

Simeon barely finishes his proclamation when

Anna approaches. Seeing Jesus, she thanks God. Anna prophesies that the baby is the expected Savior everyone is awaiting. He will redeem the people.

Just as we talked about in Days 16 and 19, Anna's thanksgiving is future-focused. She doesn't thank God for what he has done or what he is doing. She thanks God for what will be.

Jesus will grow up and redeem his people. This won't occur for over three decades. He's a baby and dependent on his parents for every aspect of his life. He's not yet ready to save anyone.

Yet Anna focuses on what our Lord will do and prophetically declares it. She thanks God that he will soon fulfill the promises he made centuries earlier.

Anna's dedication to her Lord, her prophetic words, and her thanks to God are all things that we can—and should—emulate.

Questions: *Though we are not likely in Anna's situation, what can we do to be more like her? When we look toward the future, how often do we thank God for what he will do?*

Prayer: Jesus, thank you for coming to Earth as a baby and growing up to sacrifice yourself to bring about our redemption. May we be ever mindful to thank Father God for sending you to us to save us.

DAY 21: THANK OFFERING
TODAY'S PASSAGE: LEVITICUS 7:12–15

Focus verse: "Those who sacrifice thank offerings honor me, and to the blameless I will show my salvation." (Psalm 50:23)

The law of Moses discusses giving thank offerings as an expression of thankfulness. The implication is that it's optional; it's voluntary. We can choose to give a thank offering to God or not.

The thank offering is an animal sacrifice. Accompanying it are large loaves of bread. Meat and bread provide the foundation of a meal. It belongs to the priests, but they must eat the meat on the day it's offered.

Five passages in the book of Psalms mention thank offerings. One of these psalms quotes God. He says those that sacrifice thank offerings honor him.

God continues the affirmation by saying that to the blameless he will give salvation. With these two ideas coupled together, there must be a connection.

The implication is that those who give thank offerings for the right reason—those who are blameless in their motivation—will receive salvation. (Note that this is an Old Testament promise and not a present day one.) Conversely, those who offer thank offerings with the wrong motivation will receive nothing.

When we think of thanking God, we focus on a verbal expression of appreciation. Yet a thank offering shows we can offer thanksgiving tangibly.

Though it's no longer realistic to sacrifice an animal thank offering today, as prescribed in Leviticus, we can consider practical alternatives.

The first thought is money. Though we can't directly offer God our money, we can give it to organizations aligned with him and committed to advancing his kingdom. This may be a church or parachurch organization. It could even be an individual. In any of these instances, we can equate our financial donations with a voluntary thank offering.

Next, we can sacrifice thank offerings by giving God our possessions. This should be an easy step to take if we rightly view them as his and not ours.

Another option to sacrifice thank offerings to the Lord is to give him our time. We take the time we could've used for some other activity and give it to God. It's no longer ours but his. We use this time to help others in ways that honor our Lord.

A fourth consideration to give thank offerings to God is to make things for him. This could be an art project, the result of a hobby, or the output of a business. Though we can't give them directly to our Lord, we can dedicate these things to him as we give them to others.

As with the original thank-offering sacrifice, these present-day options also loom as a sacrifice to him. We take what we have and offer it to our Lord as a voluntary expression of thanksgiving.

Questions: How willing are we to sacrifice our money, possessions, and time to give to God? How can we make sure we're giving our thank offerings with the right motivation?

Prayer: Jesus, show us how we can best offer you our sacrifice of thank offerings. May we offer them with pure hearts and grateful spirits.

DAY 22: THE THANKFUL LEPER
TODAY'S PASSAGE: LUKE 17:11–19

Focus verse: He threw himself at Jesus' feet and thanked him. (Luke 17:16)

Leprosy is an infectious skin decease that eats away flesh. It's contagious. In Jesus's day, leprosy wasn't treatable, so the goal was avoidance. People with leprosy needed to self-isolate and call out "Unclean! Unclean!" when people were near (Leviticus 13:45). This allowed others to remain at a safe distance and minimize their risk of infection.

Now let's consider today's story of ten lepers.

Jesus walks down the road. Ten lepers spot him.

Calling from a distance, they shout. "Jesus, please help us!"

The Healer gives a simple instruction: "Go and show yourself to the priests."

Though this may seem like a strange response, the law of Moses commanded people healed from a skin disease—like leprosy—to present themselves to the priests (Leviticus 14:1–32). This stands as the lepers' first step to reenter society.

The ten lepers obey Jesus. It's a step of faith. They wouldn't dare approach a priest while still infected, yet they head there anyway. They may have expected—or at least hoped—their leprosy would be gone by the time they reach the priest.

On the way, they're cleansed of their leprosy.

Upon seeing what happened, one man returns to Jesus. He praises God. He kneels before Jesus and thanks him.

Jesus commends the man but is surprised that only one leper returned to give thanks. Then the man is made well.

First, he was cleansed—they all were. Now this one man is made well.

Is there a distinction between being cleansed and being made well?

One thought is that being cleansed meant the leprosy was gone, but its ravages remained. Whereas being made well restored the flesh to its pre-leprous condition.

Another consideration is that being made well addressed the whole person, encompassing the psychological aspect of his quarantine.

Given this, it seems the man who gave thanks to Jesus—and appreciated the Healer's generosity— received more. Besides being cleansed, Jesus made him well too.

Jesus came to both heal and to save. Two thousand years ago, most people sought his healing power but missed the saving part. Today, it's often the opposite. Many people focus on his saving work but overlook the healing part. Yet Jesus does both— then and now.

Just as we thank God for saving us, we're also right to thank God for healing us.

Questions: *What do we think about Jesus healing people today? When our bodies suffer, do we turn to Jesus first or think of him last?*

Prayer: Thank you, Jesus, for saving us. Thank you, Jesus, for healing us. Just as we rely on you for our salvation, may we also rely on you for our healing.

DAY 23: MORE PSALMS OF THANKSGIVING

TODAY'S PASSAGE: PSALM 100

Focus verse: Let us come before him with thanksgiving and extol him with music and song. (Psalm 95:2)

The words *thanks* and *thanksgiving* appear twenty-two times in the book of Psalms, far more than any other book of the Bible. We've already covered several of these occurrences in Days 5, 14, and 21. Here are eight more verses from Psalms to further expand our consideration of thanksgiving.

The first four are from King David.

David sings praises and gives thanks to God

because of his righteous character (Psalm 7:17). Only our Lord is fully righteous; he always does what's right. We don't, but through Jesus we can move in that direction. This is a reason for thanksgiving.

Another time, David gives thanks to the Lord with all his heart and tells others of God's wonderful deeds (Psalm 9:1). May we likewise thank God with all our hearts. May we tell others about Jesus who has wonderfully saved us.

Third, David thanks God in the great assembly and offers praises (Psalm 35:18). This likely refers to temple gatherings, but it could be anywhere people meet. May we likewise proclaim thanksgiving and praise God to others.

Overall, David pledges to sing praises to God's name and glorify him through thanksgiving (Psalm 69:30). May our thanksgiving also glorify our Lord.

We don't know the authors of the next four psalms—numbers five through eight on our list—but that in no way lessens their meaning or impact.

Fifth, let us approach God with thanksgiving, extolling him through music (Psalm 95:2). When we approach God in prayer, may we do so with hearts overflowing with thanksgiving. In short, we open our prayers by giving thanks.

The next psalm says to "enter his gates with thanksgiving and his courts with praise" (Psalm 100:4). The gates reference the entrance to the temple and courts are areas within. In today's context, we are to enter a church with thanksgiving and praise. But do we?

Seventh is a plea for liberation so the people can return home. Then they will give thanks to God and praise him (Psalm 106:47). Thanksgiving and praise are certainly an understandable response and worthy of emulation, but why not first thank the Almighty for what he will do? Or even praise him for his presence in a difficult situation?

Last is a convicting verse. The writer pledges to get up at midnight to thank God (Psalm 119:62). This is an intentional effort. He or she will interrupt sleep to thank God. Not only should we thank God during the day but also at night, whether it's convenient or not.

Questions: *Which of these verses challenge us to give more attention to thanking God? What one action can we pledge to begin doing or to do better?*

Prayer: Holy Spirit, reveal to us how we can better offer God our thanksgiving. Remind us to be thankful when our tendency might lead us in a different direction.

DAY 24: FEEDING THE CROWD
TODAY'S PASSAGE: LUKE 9:10–17

Focus verse: Taking the five loaves and the two
fish and looking up to heaven, [Jesus] gave thanks
and broke them. Then he gave them to the disciples
to distribute to the people. (Luke 9:16)

Each of the four biographies of Jesus record when he miraculously feeds a multitude of people. It happens twice. One time there are five thousand men present. The second time there are four thousand. Matthew notes women and children are also present. This pushes the total number of people who eat Jesus's massive meal much higher, possibly over twenty-five thousand or even more.

Matthew and Mark record both events, whereas Luke and John only mention the feeding of the five thousand. This isn't because they don't care about the second time or dismiss it, but because covering one miraculous feeding may seem sufficient.

In both instances, the situation is similar. Thousands of people listen to Jesus. They've been there a long time, and they're hungry. Their food is gone. Jesus wants to feed them. He starts by taking inventory and asks his disciples, "How much food do you have?" They have little, barely enough to feed themselves.

But for Jesus, barely enough is plenty. He tells the people to sit. He takes what little food they have and, looking up to heaven, he gives thanks. Then he has his disciples pass out the food. It miraculously multiplies; everyone has enough to eat. They even have leftovers to pick up.

When Jesus thanks his heavenly Father, what is he thanking God for? Is he thanking God for the food? Or is he thanking God for the miracle of multiplying it?

When he institutes the sacrament of the Lord's Supper, he thanks God for the food (Days 18 and 28). And, as we'll also see in Day 26, Jesus thanks

God for hearing him and for the miracle that is about to happen.

For now, let's focus on thanking God for our food before we eat it. We can do this at every meal. This is a good practice that many of Jesus's followers observe.

Our prayer of thanksgiving for our food can have a threefold purpose, which likely varies with our situation.

First is thanking God that we have food to eat. Not everyone does.

Second is thanking God for the nutrition the food will provide. Not all food accomplishes this. For some people, the only staple available to fill their bellies is not healthy.

Third is thanking God for his protection that the food we ingest isn't spoiled or tainted.

We must take care, however, that our pre-meal prayer doesn't become a requisite ritual to complete or a mindless mumbling to rush through. Keeping each prayer fresh and meaningful becomes even more challenging over time, given that we could do it more than one thousand times every year.

Yet, we must try. God deserves nothing less. We should give him our best, offering him a heartfelt thanksgiving for the food we eat.

Questions: What do we think about following Jesus's example of thanking God for our food? How can we eat in a way that honors our provider?

Prayer: Lord, thank you for the food you provide. May we never presume your provision, and may we always eat with heartfelt gratitude.

DAY 25: JOY AND GLADNESS
TODAY'S PASSAGE: ISAIAH 51:1–16

Focus verse: Joy and gladness will be found in her, thanksgiving and the sound of singing. (Isaiah 51:3)

The passage in Isaiah 51 comes to the people amid difficult times. They struggle; they're discouraged. God's promises seem far away, improbable to realize.

Isaiah offers them comfort. He has them recall the past. God made them in his image. They are descendants of Abraham and Sarah. From one man came many—an entire nation. Just as God comforted Abraham and Sarah in their old age before Isaac was born, he will comfort his people now. He sees the ruins. He will turn the deserts into

Eden, a garden for God springing from the wastelands.

Joy and gladness will return to his people once again. Then they will offer thanksgiving and sing songs to the Lord.

Isaiah continues his encouragement by talking about justice, salvation, and hope. God's salvation will last eternally. His righteousness will never let them down. And they can hope in him.

Isaiah calls them to awake and get ready. Just as God provided for his people in the past, he'll do so again. Isaiah returns to God's promise of joy and gladness, mentioning it a second time to remind the people of the Lord's pledge (Isaiah 51:11).

Joy and gladness may be a regular part of our lives now. Or joy and gladness may only be a memory from long ago. Perhaps joy and gladness have always been distant.

Yet we should take comfort in knowing our Lord wants us to experience lives of joy. He wants us to have gladness in our hearts. The result of joy and gladness is thanksgiving and singing.

If we have joy and gladness in our hearts now, may we thank God and sing our praises to him. Yet if we lack these outcomes in our present lives, may we thank God and sing praises to him because he remembers us and wants to provide us with these two gifts.

There seems, however, to be a prerequisite to receiving God's joy and gladness. We find it in verse one of Isaiah 51. Isaiah directs his words to those who pursue righteousness.

But Isaiah isn't telling us we must be righteous, merely that we pursue it. We need to move toward it.

In the Old Testament, righteousness was how the people earned their salvation—or at least how they could strive to earn it. In truth, it was an impossible goal to achieve.

Yet through Jesus we don't need to earn our salvation. We merely need to believe in him and follow him. When we put our trust in Jesus for our lives and for our eternity, he makes us righteous. Because of Jesus, Father God sees our right-eousness. This is even though we presently fall short of the righteous ideals that God desires for us to have.

When we follow Jesus as his disciple, we move closer to this righteousness day by day. We pursue right living. This isn't to earn our salvation—or even keep it. Instead, it's a way of thanking God for the salvation he has already provided to us through

Jesus.

Questions: *Do we have joy and gladness in our lives? Regardless of our answer, what should we do? More importantly, do we have Jesus in our lives? How should we respond?*

Prayer: Heavenly Father, may we experience the joy and gladness you promise. Jesus, may we receive in faith the salvation you provide. Thank you!

DAY 26: LAZARUS

TODAY'S PASSAGE: JOHN 11:1–44

Focus verse: Jesus looked up and said, "Father, I thank you that you have heard me. I knew that you always hear me, but I said this for the benefit of the people standing here, that they may believe that you sent me." (John 11:41–42).

J esus loves the siblings Martha, Mary, and Lazarus. He sometimes goes to their house. The sisters send word that Lazarus is sick. But Jesus doesn't leave to heal his ailing friend. He tarries. "Don't worry," he tells his disciples. "Lazarus's sickness won't lead to death but is to glorify me."

Jesus waits two days before heading out. "Lazarus is sleeping," he says, "and I'm going to wake him."

The disciples assume this means Lazarus is getting better.

Jesus corrects their wrong thinking. "Lazarus is dead." He tells his disciples it was good for them he wasn't there when it happened. "This will help you believe. Let's go to him."

As Jesus and his followers near the city where Lazarus once lived, Martha runs out to meet him. "If you had been here," she says, "he wouldn't have died. But even now, I know God will answer your prayers."

Jesus promises Martha that Lazarus will rise again.

She agrees but assumes Jesus means her brother will rise to life on the last day.

"I am the resurrection, and I am the life," Jesus says. "If you believe in me, you will never die."

Martha confirms she believes and leaves to find Mary.

Mary reaches Jesus, with a throng of mourners trailing her. She falls before him. "If you'd been here, he wouldn't have died."

Moved in his spirit and troubled, Jesus asks, "Where's he buried?"

They take him to Lazarus's tomb.

Jesus cries.

He commands them to roll away the stone sealing the grave's entrance.

But before God does anything, before God answers Jesus's prayer, Jesus gives thanks. "Father, I thank you that you heard me. You always hear me."

Besides thanking God for hearing his prayer, Jesus implicitly thanks him for the miracle that's about to happen.

"Lazarus," Jesus commands, "come out."

The once-dead Lazarus staggers out of his tomb, burial linens still wrapped around his body. How shocking to see the formerly dead man lumber forth. It's certainly worthy of thanking God.

Questions: *When we pray, do we believe God hears? Do we thank the Almighty for answering our prayers before we realize the outcome?*

Prayer: Lord God, thank you for hearing our prayers. May we also thank you in advance for your answers to our prayers. And even if we don't realize the answer we seek, may we still thank you in faith, knowing that you have a better plan in mind.

DAY 27: PROFESSIONALS

TODAY'S PASSAGE: 2 CHRONICLES 31:1–8

Focus verse: Hezekiah assigned the priests and Levites . . . to offer burnt offerings and fellowship offerings, to minister, to give thanks and to sing praises at the gates of the Lord's dwelling.

(2 Chronicles 31:2)

With the nation of Israel conquered, only Judah remains. Though they mostly struggle to obey God, just as Israel struggled, King Hezekiah takes a God-honoring approach and institutes needed reforms.

First, he purifies the temple (2 Chronicles 29). Next, he celebrates the Passover in grand fashion (2 Chronicles 30).

Then, with much zeal, the people go throughout the land and destroy all forms of worship that oppose God and are contrary to putting him first and serving him only. We read about this in today's passage.

Last, King Hezekiah clarifies his expectations for the priests and Levites, according to their assigned duties.

They are to offer burnt offerings and fellowship offerings. This implicitly falls to the priests, since the rest of the Levites are prohibited from doing this.

They are also to give thanks and sing praises at the temple. Though this could apply to the priests as well, we assume this falls to the Levites. Though Moses had assigned the Levites to transport the tabernacle and items relating to worship, King David had reassigned them "to extol, thank, and praise the LORD" (1 Chronicles 16:4). This was a reasonable decision since their original task no longer existed.

In stating his expectations, King Hezekiah simply reminds the priests and the Levites to do what they should've been doing all along.

They are professional clergy. The priests attend to the sacrifices, and the Levites focus on giving thanks and singing praises. It's their job. It's what they're paid to do.

This doesn't mean, however, that if we pay people to thank God and sing praises to him, that we don't have to. We must do it too. We should want to.

Professionals can lead us in worship, but the emphasis is on leading. Through their example, we can better thank and sing praises to God. Paid professionals merely help us do so better—or at least they should. They're to lead us in worship, not replace us in worship.

We must take an active part and not sit idly as we watch others worship for us. May we never forget to thank God and sing our praises to him.

If we work as a professional to worship God, may we do so to the best of our ability and for his glory—not for applause or adulation.

If we aren't professional worshipers, may we never forget that we should still do our best to thank God and sing our praises to him.

He deserves nothing less.

Questions: *What is our attitude toward people who lead* *us in worship? What must we change to make sure we're actively giving thanks to God and singing our praises?*

Prayer: Heavenly Father, may we always be mindful to give you thanks and sing our praises to you. May we do so whether others lead us or not. May we do so when we're at church and when we're not—especially when we're not. We ask this in Jesus's name.

DAY 28: PASSOVER BECOMES THE LORD'S SUPPER

TODAY'S PASSAGE: LUKE 22:7–20

Focus verse: After taking the cup, he gave thanks and said, "Take this and divide it among you."
(Luke 22:17)

In the book of Exodus, we read about God's people who are slaves in Egypt. God is orchestrating their release. Through a series of plagues, with increasing devastation, the Almighty is getting Pharaoh's attention.

Before the tenth and final plague, God gives his people some specific instructions (Exodus 12:1–14). Each family is to take a lamb—one without defect —and slaughter it. They're to spread the lamb's blood on the sides and tops of their doorframes.

Then they're to roast the lamb and eat it as a family.

That night, God promises to go throughout Egypt and kill the firstborn of every family that doesn't have lamb's blood on their doorframes. But he'll pass over the homes with blood on them. They call this day Passover, because death passed over their homes. They're to celebrate it every year to remember what God did to save them and deliver them.

After this first Passover—and the death it caused in the Egyptian households—Pharaoh lets the people go. They're free at last.

Now let's jump ahead several centuries to Jesus and his disciples. It's time for the annual Passover celebration. Jesus wants to celebrate it with his disciples. Peter and John make the needed preparations to commemorate this annual event.

That evening, Jesus gathers with his disciples. He's eager to share the Passover meal with them because he's about to give the Passover celebration a new meaning, one with eternal consequences.

Jesus will soon sacrifice himself on their behalf —and ours. This is to atone for our sins—to cover our lifetime of mistakes, both past and future.

Just as the lambs' blood in the Old Testament

spared the Hebrew people from death and brought about their deliverance from slavery, so, too, with Jesus as our Lamb—the ultimate sacrifice. His sacrifice, represented by his blood, spares us from death and brings about our deliverance from sin.

When Jesus celebrates the Passover with his disciples, he expands its meaning. He turns it into the Lord's Supper, also known as Communion or the Eucharist. Each time we celebrate the Lord's Supper, we remember Jesus's sacrificial death to save us and his resurrection from the grave to give us eternal life.

Just as Jesus thanked the Father for the wine and the bread at this first Lord's Supper, so, too, should we thank Jesus for dying to save us.

Questions: *What does Jesus's sacrificial death mean to us? What should our response be? How can our celebration of the Lord's Supper help us better remember Jesus?*

Prayer: Jesus, thank you for loving us and sacrificing yourself to save us. We praise you for who you are and what you did. May we never grow tired of telling others about you. Amen.

DAY 29: VICTORY THROUGH JESUS
TODAY'S PASSAGE: 1 CORINTHIANS 15:54–58

Focus verse: But thanks be to God! He gives us
the victory through our Lord Jesus Christ.
(1 Corinthians 15:57)

The word *victory* appears three times in today's passage. The first two occurrences draw from the Old Testament.

Paul writes that victory has swallowed up death. This paraphrases Isaiah 25:8, which says that God will swallow up death forever. It sounds a lot like victory. In doing so, our Lord will wipe away our tears and remove our disgrace. Today, we see our victory over death coming to us through our Lord Jesus Christ. Thanks be to God for his amazing gift.

Next, Paul restates Hosea 13:14. In it, Paul seems to taunt death, asking where is your victory? Where is your sting? Hosea, however, uses different words. Instead of victory, he talks about deliverance. Instead of sting, he mentions plagues and destruction. Yet the intent of both passages is the same. God will deliver us and give us victory—through our Lord Jesus Christ.

Both Isaiah and Hosea look toward the future. They envision a victory that will one day occur. To make sure we don't miss it, Paul confirms God gave us victory through our Lord Jesus Christ. For this, we give our thanks to God.

Solomon teaches that though we may prepare for battle, the "victory rests with the LORD" (Proverbs 21:31). We must turn to the Almighty if we hope to receive his victory. This includes turning to Jesus to receive his salvation.

The theme of victory recurs throughout the book of Psalms. In its last appearance, the psalmist writes that God "delights in his people" and "crowns the humble with victory" (Psalm 149:4).

Humility, after all, is how we approach God. We humbly come to him and put our trust in Jesus to save us. We don't try to save ourselves; we can't.

Yet we will have victory—we do have victory—through our Lord Jesus Christ.

Elsewhere in the New Testament, Matthew quotes another of Isaiah's prophecies about Jesus, that the coming Savior will not give up until he has brought complete victory (Matthew 12:19–21). Isaiah frames this as justice (Isaiah 42:1–4).

Furthermore, the apostle John writes that through Jesus we will take part in the victory that has overcome the world (1 John 5:3–5). For this we give thanks to our Lord Jesus Christ.

Questions: *What does victory through Jesus look like? What can we do to better thank Jesus for the victory he provides?*

Prayer: Jesus, thank you for giving us victory. May we tell others about you and help grow your kingdom.

DAY 30: THANK THE LORD GOD ALMIGHTY

TODAY'S PASSAGE: REVELATION 11:15–19

Focus verse: "We give thanks to you, Lord God Almighty, the One who is and who was, because you have taken your great power and have begun to reign." (Revelation 11:17)

For our final reading in *Thanksgiving with Jesus*, it seems fitting to end with the final book of the Bible. It's the apostle John's epic revelation about the end times.

John's prophetic vision, however, need not overwhelm us. Here's a succinct overview: At the end of time, a last battle will occur between good and evil. God wins. The end.

Given this, it's appropriate to give thanks to

God for what he will accomplish, which will usher us into a new heaven and a new earth where we will live with him forever.

Three passages in John's future-focused vision talk about giving thanks to God.

We begin with the four living creatures who never stop saying, "Holy, holy, holy is the Lord God Almighty, who was, and is, and is to come" (Revelation 4:8); they're quoting Isaiah 6:3. In response to their praise and thanksgiving, the twenty-four elders fall down and also worship God (Revelation 4:9–10).

Later, the angels standing around God's throne likewise fall on their faces and worship God. "Amen! Praise and glory and wisdom and thanks and honor and power and strength be to our God for ever and ever. Amen!" (Revelation 7:11–12).

Last, the twenty-four elders seated on their thrones before God likewise fall on their faces to worship him. "We give thanks to you, Lord God Almighty, the One who is and who was, because you have taken your great power and have begun to reign" (Revelation 11:16–17).

Why, we may wonder, are the four living crea-tures, the angels, and the twenty-four elders all giving thanks to Father God instead of Jesus? It is, after all, Jesus who saves us.

First, remember that Jesus and the Father are one (John 17:11, 22). Even if we struggle to grasp what this means, thanking one also thanks the other.

Second, recall that Jesus said he is the way (John 14:6). He is not the destination. The Father is the destination. It's Jesus who provides the way for us to connect with Father God.

Third, Jesus is present at the end of this age. We will live with him in the great city forever (Revelation 22:12–17).

Thank you, Jesus, for what you did to save us, for what you're doing in our lives today, and that you'll be with us forever.

Thank you, Holy Spirit, for living in us (1 Corinthians 3:16) and reminding us of all that Jesus taught (John 14:26).

Thank you, Father God, for your plan—from the very beginning—for your Son to save us and make this all happen (1 Peter 1:20).

Questions: *What do we think about the Father and the Son being one? What do we think about praying to the* *various parts of the godhead as we have done throughout this book?*

Prayer: Father, Son, and Holy Spirit, we give you all our praise and all our thanksgiving. Without you, we are nothing. You redeemed and restored us into a right relationship with you, as it was at the beginning of creation. Just as Adam walked with you in the cool of the day, may we anticipate walking with you throughout eternity.

If you liked *Thanksgiving with Jesus,* please leave a review online. Your review will help others discover this book and encourage them to read it too.

Thank you.

BOOKS IN THE HOLIDAY
CELEBRATION DEVOTIONAL SERIES

Which devotional do you want to read next?

- The Advent of Jesus
- The Passion of Jesus (Lent)
- The Victory of Jesus (Easter)
- The Ministry of Jesus
- Thanksgiving with Jesus
- New Year with Jesus

Be the first to hear about Peter's new books and receive updates at PeterDeHaan.com/updates.

IF YOU'RE NEW TO THE BIBLE

Each entry in this book contains Bible references. These can guide you if you want to learn more. If you're not familiar with the Bible, here's an overview to get you started, give some context, and minimize confusion.

First, the Bible is a collection of works written by various authors over several centuries. Think of the Bible as a diverse anthology of godly communication. It contains historical accounts, poetry, songs, letters of instruction and encouragement, messages from God sent through his representatives, and prophecies.

Most versions of the Bible have sixty-six books grouped into two sections: The Old Testament and the New Testament. The Old Testament contains thirty-nine books that precede and anticipate Jesus. The New Testament includes twenty-seven books and covers Jesus's life and the work of his followers.

The reference notations in the Bible, such as Romans 3:23, are analogous to line numbers in a Shakespearean play. They serve as a study aid. Since the Bible is much longer and more complex than a play, its reference notations are more involved.

As already mentioned, the Bible is an amalgam of books, or sections, such as Genesis, Psalms, or Matthew. These are the names given to them, over time, based on the piece's author, audience, or purpose.

In the 1200s, each book was divided into chapters, such as Acts 2 or Psalm 23. In the 1500s, the chapters were further subdivided into verses, such as John 3:16. Let's use this as an example.

The name of the book (John) appears first, followed by the chapter number (3), a colon, and then the verse number (16). Sometimes called a chapter-verse reference notation, this helps people quickly find a specific text regardless of their version of the Bible.

Although the goal was to place these chapter and verse divisions at logical breaks, they sometimes seem arbitrary. Therefore, it's good practice to read what precedes and follows each passage you're studying. The text before or after it may contain relevant insights into the portion you're exploring.

Here's how to look up a specific passage in the Bible based on its reference: Most Bibles contain a table of contents, which gives the page number for the beginning of each book. Start there. Locate the book you want to read, and turn to that page. Then flip forward to the chapter you want. Last, skim that chapter to locate the specific verse.

If you want to read online, enter the reference into BibleGateway.com or BibleHub.com. Also check out the YouVersion Bible App.

Learn more about the greatest book ever written at ABibleADay.com, which provides a Bible blog, summaries of the books of the Bible, a dictionary of Bible terms, Bible reading plans, and other resources.

ABOUT PETER DEHAAN

Peter DeHaan, PhD, wants to change the world one word at a time. His books and blog posts discuss God, the Bible, and church, geared toward spiritual seekers and church dropouts. Many people feel church has let them down, and Peter seeks to encourage them as they search for a place to belong.

But he's not afraid to ask tough questions or make religious people squirm. He's not trying to be provocative. Instead, he seeks truth, even if it makes people uncomfortable. Peter urges Christians to push past the status quo and reexamine how they practice their faith in every part of their lives.

Peter earned his doctorate, awarded with high distinction, from Trinity College of the Bible and Theological Seminary. He lives with his wife in beautiful Southwest Michigan and wrangles cross-word puzzles in his spare time.

A lifelong student of Scripture, Peter wrote the 1,000-page website ABibleADay.com to encourage people to explore the Bible, the greatest book ever written. His popular blog addresses biblical Christianity to build a faith that matters.

Read his blog, receive his newsletter, and learn more at PeterDeHaan.com.

BOOKS BY PETER DEHAAN

Holiday Celebration Devotionals

The Advent of Jesus

The Passion of Jesus (Lent)

The Victory of Jesus (Easter)

The Ministry of Jesus

Thanksgiving with Jesus

New Year with Jesus

40-Day Bible Study Series

Dear Theophilus (the Gospel of Luke)

Acts Bible Study

Isaiah Bible Study

Minor Prophets Bible Study

Job Bible Study

Living Water (John)

Love Is Patient (1 and 2 Corinthians)

Revelation Bible Study

1, 2, & 3 John Bible Study

Hebrews Bible Study

James and Jude Bible Study

Matthew Bible Study

1 & 2 Peter Bible Study

Mark Bible Study

Bible Character Sketches Series

Women of the Bible

The Friends and Foes of Jesus

Old Testament Sinners and Saints

More Old Testament Sinners and Saints

Heroes and Heavies of the Apocrypha

200 Old Testament Sinners and Saints

Visiting Churches Series

52 Churches

The 52 Churches Workbook

More Than 52 Churches

The More Than 52 Churches Workbook

Visiting Online Church

Other Books

Elephant God

Jesus's Broken Church

Martin Luther's 95 Theses (formerly *95 Tweets*)

The Christian Church's LGBTQ Failure

Bridging the Sacred-Secular Divide (*Woodpecker Wars*)

Beyond Psalm 150

How Big Is Your Tent?

For the latest list of all Peter's books, go to PeterDeHaan.com/books.

www.ingramcontent.com/pod-product-compliance
Lightning Source LLC
Chambersburg PA
CBHW061650120626
46550CB00003B/887